Night/Times

Chelsea Riley

Presentation by *BookLeaf Publishing*

Web: www.bookleafpub.com

E-mail: info@bookleafpub.com

ISBN: 978-93-5774-391-4

First edition 2023

Senseless : A Haiku

Alone in the dark
I throw my heart out with force
But no gravity.

Wings at Dusk

She drew her wings on herself everyday
And always by dusk, they'd wash away

Regardless of any armor she'd wear,
No Man or no Creature could eventually spare

The blows so forceful in various form
Like harsh destruction of a vengeful storm

The thunder resounding a path through her head
The raindrops piercing with pain from undead

She opened her arms and looked up with a grin
As the squall twisted and drew her in

And so the drew on her wings one final day
As everyone watched

She had flown away.

Time&Space

OnedayIwillfinallydedicatethetimetoallowmysel
fspacefromallofthepperniciousinfluencesinmylife
butIsupposeitisapparentthattodayisnotthatday.

Wait in the Night

Silently patient
Beneath the moonlight
I sit alone
And wait in the night

The coldness comes
And chills my spine
Darkness wrapping my eyes
And making me blind

I breathe out slow
Under street lights dimmed
And listen for you
In the whispering wind

Only in darkness
I see your guidance
Hearing you clearly
In the night's silence.

I long for peace.
Inspiration to write.
And here you find me
While I wait in the night.

Full Moon: Haiku

Her platinum smile,
She's a sign of the harvest
Greeting the night's chill.

Weight in the Night

I awaken
Hoping to feel refreshed
But instead
I feel a weight on my chest

With labored breath
I try as I might
But I can't even shift
To my left or my right

Now is certainly not
The time to panic
Things will only be worse
If I become frantic

It's time to move
Like the telling clock does,
So using my hands
I feel the soft fuzz.

And I lift the weight
Now slightly askew
My consequence now,
A slightly faint "mew."

Oh, the worry!
You thought the weight was just that.
When it was all but just
My sleeping cat.

Pillow Talk: Haiku

I woke up and asked,
"Why are you looking at me?"
…He called me Gorgeous.

To: Kris

Doom

The nightly resident
Her name is Doom
She sits in the corner
With darkness and gloom

Dark as the shadows
She shares in her nook
Sending chills down your back
With one single look

She won't move an inch
Yet neither will you
Still in the corner
The whole night through

So what if Doom
Is misperceived
And not the Demon
You want to believe?

Rather a soul
That feels your doom,
And guard off demons
From rushing the room

So close your eyes
Let your slumber begin,
And Doom will keep watch
Once you're tucked tightly in.

Recurring Nightmare: Haiku

When I dreamt of you
You were under the water
And I could not sink

Good Morning, Night

Alone in the dark
I glance all around
But there is no light
Not even a sound.

I could sleep again
Try as I might,
But now it's no use.
Good morning, Night.

A battle is here
Such a warm cozy bed
With a warm lazy body
And a fast busy head.

My dreams turn to questions
And questions won't stop
My mind searches for answers
And spins like a top.

There is no pain.
Not even a fright,
Just one of those times.
Good morning, Night.

Try it again
I know the price if I don't.
I could still get some sleep…
…

…

…

But probably won't.

I could maybe count sheep.
Perhaps take a stroll,
Or pick up my phone
Like a nocturnal troll.

So I'm cuddling blankets
I'll curl into a ball
Hoping the Sandman
Can hear my call.

But the night has its beauty
In the air a low hum.
I share my secrets
Including this poem.

Let's try to sleep now
And not ruminate
But suddenly darkness
Will now illuminate.

Creeping in on our secrets
Comes slithering light
Farewell, Darkness
It's been alright.

I guess what I mean to say is
…Good Night…

* 9 7 8 9 3 5 7 7 4 3 9 1 4 *